Get Ready for ROBOTS!

by Patricia Lauber

illustrated by True Kelley

HarperCollinsPublishers

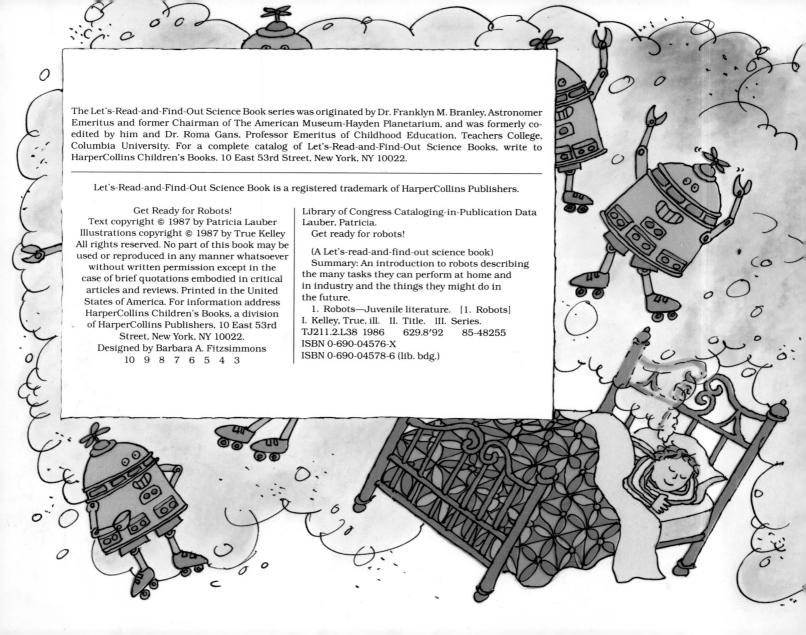

The Let's-Read-and-Find-Out Science Book series was originated by Dr. Franklyn M. Branley, Astronomer Emeritus and former Chairman of The American Museum-Hayden Planetarium, and was formerly co-edited by him and Dr. Roma Gans, Professor Emeritus of Childhood Education, Teachers College, Columbia University. For a complete catalog of Let's-Read-and-Find-Out Science Books, write to HarperCollins Children's Books, 10 East 53rd Street, New York, NY 10022.

Let's-Read-and-Find-Out Science Book is a registered trademark of HarperCollins Publishers.

Library of Congress Cataloging-in-Publication Data
Lauber, Patricia.
  Get ready for robots!

  (A Let's-read-and-find-out science book)
  Summary: An introduction to robots describing the many tasks they can perform at home and in industry and the things they might do in the future.
  1. Robots—Juvenile literature. [1. Robots]
I. Kelley, True, ill. II. Title. III. Series.
TJ211.2.L38 1986   629.8'92   85-48255
ISBN 0-690-04576-X
ISBN 0-690-04578-6 (lib. bdg.)

You are having a wonderful dream about a robot that can

set the table,

make your bed,

make a sandwich,

hang up your clothes,

play games,

mow the grass.

3

Someday you may have a robot like that. Many people may. But right now that robot is only a dream. The clever robots you see in movies are not really robots at all. Most have a person inside, doing things that only human beings can do. Real robots are very different.

The Turtle is a robot that rolls around on wheels. It has a pen under its belly that it uses for drawing. It can draw squares, circles, and other shapes with the pen. It can explore a room and then draw a small map of it.

You might meet a Turtle in school or in a friend's home.

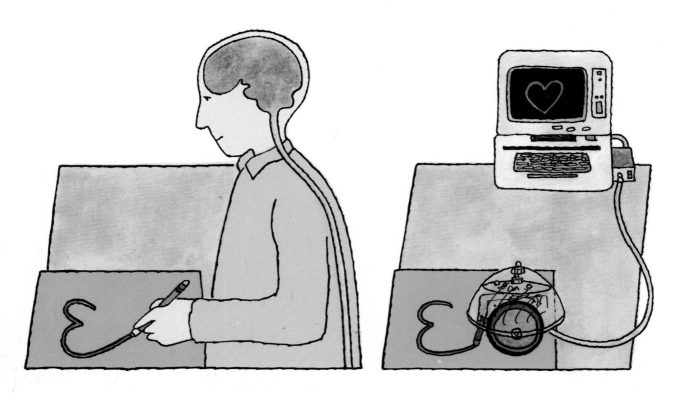

Like other robots, the Turtle has a body that is a machine. It has a computer for a brain.

In a human being the brain tells the body what to do. In a robot the computer tells the machine what to do.

The Turtle's computer sends signals through a cable. The signals make the machine move. They make it draw. The machine follows the instructions without human help.

Humans put the instructions into the computer. They may give it a whole set of instructions, which is called a program. Or they may type instructions one by one on the computer keyboard.

This Turtle is finding its way through a maze. Like most robots, the Turtle cannot see. But it can feel things. The machine has feelers under its shell. They are called sensors. They sense when the machine bumps into something and send signals back to the computer.

The computer keeps track of places where the machine had to turn or back off. It uses this information to make a kind of map of the maze. Next time, the Turtle can find its way without bumping into anything.

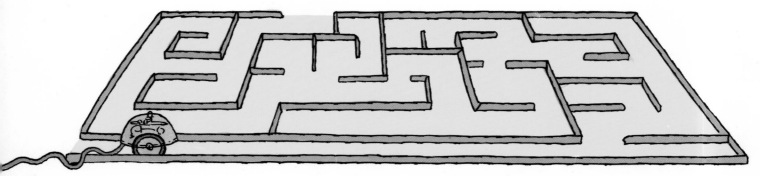

RB5X is a small home robot that also wheels around bumping into things and making a map. Unlike the Turtle, it has a tiny, built-in computer. A program in the computer tells RB5X what to do.

RB5X runs on electricity, as do other robots. It has a battery. When the power runs down, RB5X plugs itself in and charges up its battery.

Some home robots can sense people or things without bumping into them. They turn away before hitting anything.

Some obey spoken commands.

Some can speak. They have something called a voice synthesizer. It changes computer signals into sounds that make words.

Home robots are fun, but so far they do not do much work around the house. Most of the robots that really work have jobs in factories.

Which one of these is the robot?

If you guessed the big metal arm, you guessed
right. It is a robot that works in a factory. Its job is
to spray paint. That is a good job for a robot to do.

When paint is being sprayed, the workroom air fills with tiny paint droplets. These can harm a person's lungs, eyes, and skin. So human workers may need to wear spacesuits, which are hot and awkward. A robot doesn't need a suit. It doesn't breathe air, and it has no eyes or skin.

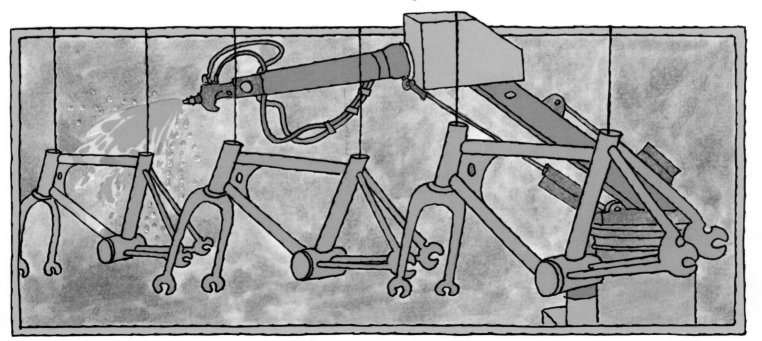

Factory robots do jobs that are hard, boring, dirty, or dangerous for people. Many factory robots join pieces of metal together, using the heat of a torch—they do welding. Some lift heavy weights all day, without having to rest.

Robots probably helped to make your family's refrigerator, washing machine, or car.

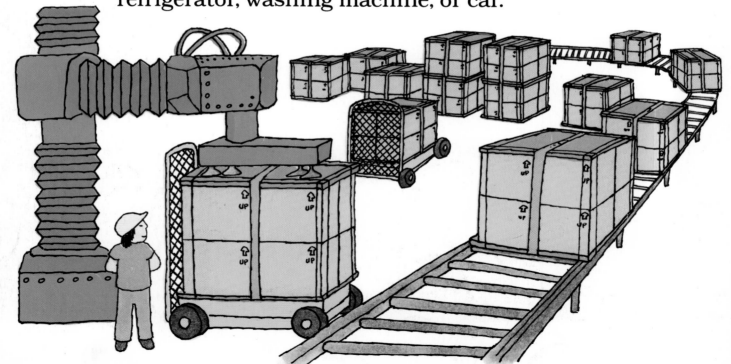

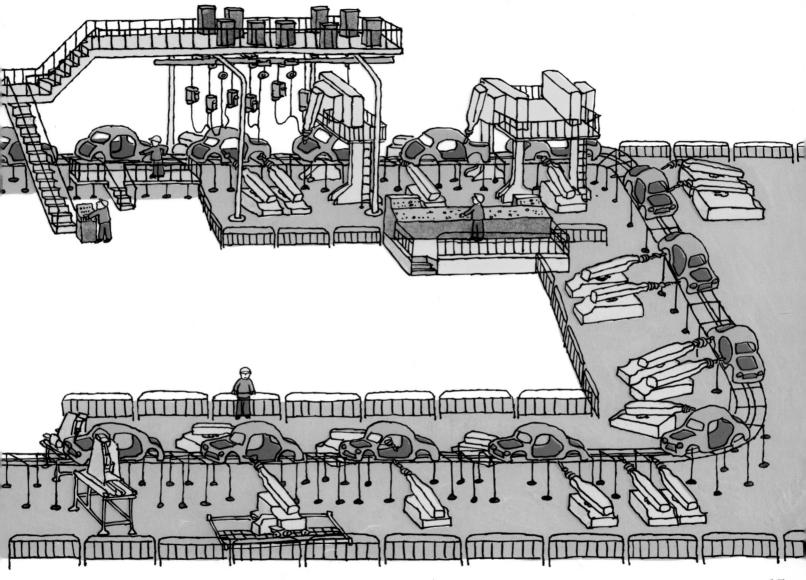

15

There are robots that can do still other
kinds of work. One kind of robot works as a
lumberjack. It uses a set of wheels to climb trees,
going round and round the tree trunks. It trims
off branches with a chain saw.

Another robot cleans the outsides of ships. It can work underwater. There it scrubs off small plants and animals, like barnacles, that grow on the bottoms of ships and slow them down.

Robot guards work nights in factories and other buildings. If they sense smoke, heat, escaping gas, or a moving person, they send out an alarm. Some home robots can do these things too.

Someday soon you may see robots at work in airport lobbies and supermarkets. They will vacuum carpeting and wash floors. Lobbies and markets are good places for robots to clean. They are big, open spaces, where no one moves the chairs and shelves around.

In the future, robots may help fight fires, paint high bridges, wash the windows of skyscrapers, and do other dangerous jobs.

Robots cannot see the way people see. If they could, they could do many more things. In a human being, the eyes send signals to the brain. The brain makes sense of the signals—and the person sees. In a robot, TV cameras can send signals to the computer. But the computer has a hard time making sense of the signals.

You, for example, know a table when you see one. But what is a table? Do you tell by the shape? By the number of legs? If someone is sitting on it, is it still a table? You know. But how can you explain all you know about tables to a computer?

Some new robots can make sense out of certain things that their TV eyes see. For example, they see well enough to make typewriter keyboards, lift boxes from moving carts,

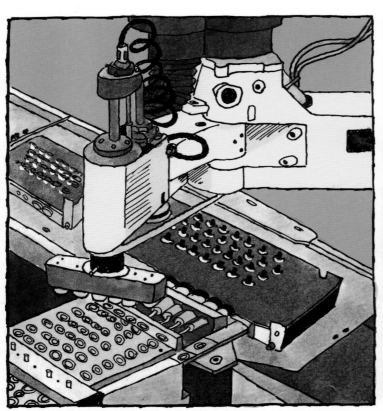

and put glue on the edges of car windshields and fit them in place.

Even so, these robots do not see nearly as well as people do.

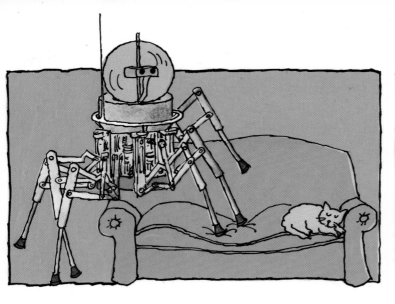
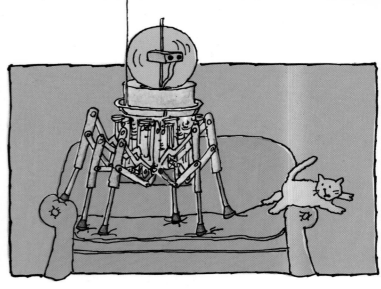

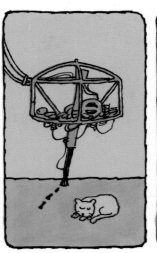
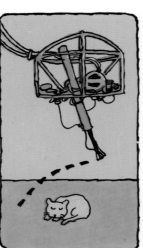
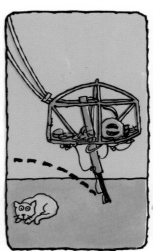

Robots could also do more things if they had legs instead of wheels. They could climb stairs. They could travel over very rough ground. They could go almost anywhere.

Walking machines are hard to build, but a few have been made. One, a crawling machine, has six legs like an insect, for good balance. A built-in computer decides which legs are to move. Another one is a hopping machine, a kind of pogo stick. If the hopper starts to tip, a built-in computer quickly balances it.

Both these machines are steered by people nearby and are not true robots. But they may lead to robots that can walk, run, or jump, and can go places where robots on wheels cannot go.

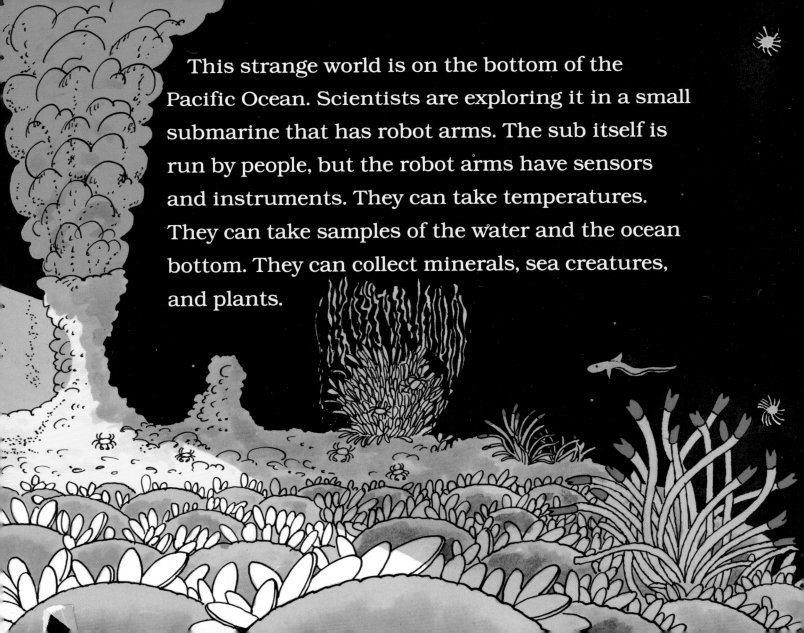

This strange world is on the bottom of the
Pacific Ocean. Scientists are exploring it in a small
submarine that has robot arms. The sub itself is
run by people, but the robot arms have sensors
and instruments. They can take temperatures.
They can take samples of the water and the ocean
bottom. They can collect minerals, sea creatures,
and plants.

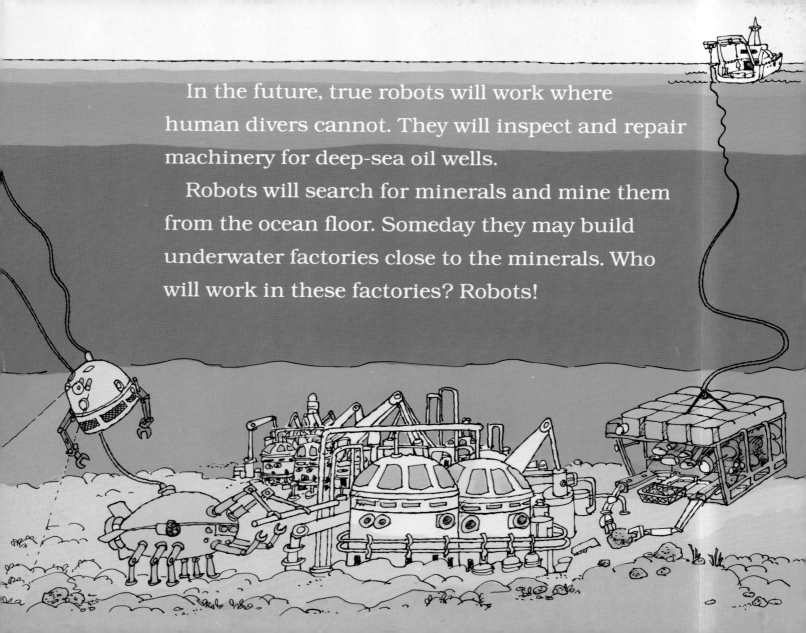

In the future, true robots will work where human divers cannot. They will inspect and repair machinery for deep-sea oil wells.

Robots will search for minerals and mine them from the ocean floor. Someday they may build underwater factories close to the minerals. Who will work in these factories? Robots!

Robots have worked in space for many years.
Some satellites and space probes are really robots.
Their computer brains fire their rockets
automatically to keep them in the right path. The
computers also send information and photos to
Earth.

In 1976 two robots parachuted from their spacecraft onto Mars. There they measured wind direction and speed, listened for marsquakes, and took soil samples. All the time, the robots were millions of miles from any human being.

Space is a good place to use robots. They don't need air, food, water, doctors, vacations, or their families.

Someday you will see robots repairing satellites, mining other planets, and building space factories. You may even see robots setting out on voyages to the stars—voyages that will last longer than a human lifetime.

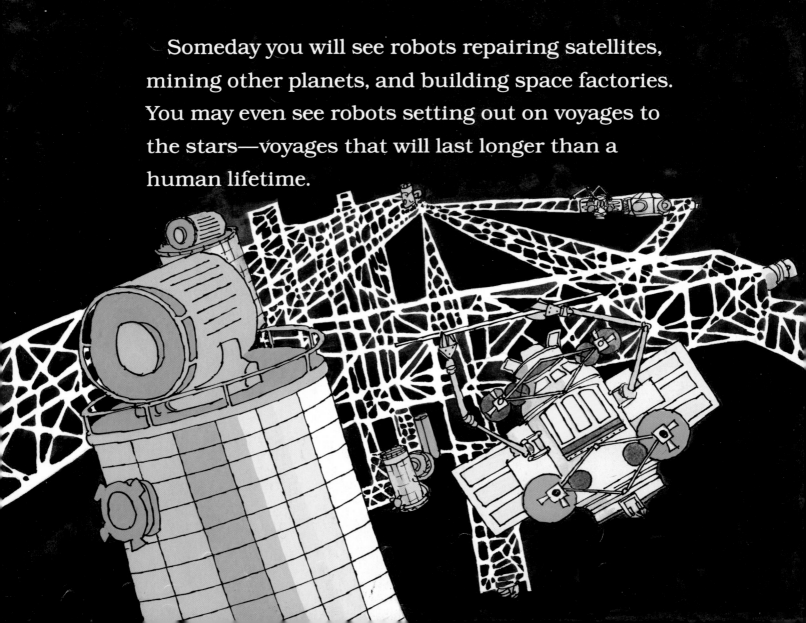

You are having a wonderful dream. You have invented a robot that can save lives.

Someday you might do that. And this is one big difference between people and robots. Robots can only do what people teach them to do. But *you* can dream big dreams, set goals, and reach them if you really try.